Remaining Faithful

A Guide for Reflecting on Short-Term Mission Experiences

A manual for reflection, integration and prayer
after a short-term experience in another culture

JULIE LUPIEN and MICHELLE A. SCHEIDT

**From Mission
to Mission**

A Resource for Mission and Transition

Our Mission

From Mission to Mission assists people in the preparation and processing of their cross-cultural, ministerial, and life transitions to continue their Christian call to mission.

Remaining Faithful: A Guide for Reflecting on Short-Term Mission Experiences
    by Julie Lupien and Michelle A. Scheidt, DMin
ISBN 978-0-9983160-2-4
Second edition copyright ©2017 by **From Mission to Mission** Society
Originally published as *Remaining Faithful: How Do I Keep My Experience Alive?*
First edition copyright ©2005 by **From Mission to Mission** Society

From Mission
to Mission

missiontomission.org

Remaining Faithful

A Guide for Reflecting on Short-Term Mission Experiences

This book is published by the nonprofit organization **From Mission to Mission**.

In 1980 **From Mission to Mission** was created to offer support to returning missioners and volunteers as they deal with the unique transition of re-entry. As missioners ourselves, we understand the situations and life struggles experienced in mission that are virtually unknown here at home. We know the challenge of returning to a place you once called home and seeing it with a new vision that has been shaped by your experience in another culture. We also share the struggle to be faithful to the values, attitudes and insights acquired during the cross-cultural experience. **From Mission to Mission** seeks to help returned missioners and volunteers live mission here in their home culture, in a way that honors those to whom they have said goodbye.

From Mission to Mission aims to offer support for all returning missioners and volunteers, no matter from where they return, or for how long they have served. This includes:

- Lay missioners and volunteers, religious sisters, priests and brothers, diocesan priests;
- Those who have served from a few days to those who have served for decades;
- International and domestic missioners and volunteers.

We offer publications, workshops, consultations, and other resources; see page 64 for details. **From Mission to Mission** is available to assist you at any time by phone, Skype, email, or in person with issues that arise related to trauma, whether you are an individual volunteer or missioner, a family or community member, the leader of an organization or community. Wherever you are in your mission journey, please contact us if you need support related to any aspect of re-entry.

—From Mission to Mission

We dedicate this book to all the people in the world we have gone to serve and from whom we received many more gifts in return.

Special thanks to:

Ellen Belle

Bonita Bock

Gerry Doran

Bill Jaster

Mary Frances Jaster

Maureen McNamee

From Mission to Mission Board of Directors and the many others who offered suggestions and advice

We are grateful to the Sisters of Loretto of Denver, Colorado, and the Franciscan Sisters of Oldenburg, Indiana, whose financial support helped us to initiate this project.

Table of Contents

Table of Contents

How to Use This Resource

Remaining Faithful is a resource that can be used in a variety of ways to best fit your needs. The important thing is to reflect on the experience you had and let your reflection influence the choices you make in life.

"Experience is not the best teacher. We learn nothing from experience. We only learn from reflection of experience."—Tony Saddington

Suggestions on how to use *Remaining Faithful*:

- For groups who meet regularly after returning from a short-term experience, we suggest following the manual as it was written, using the monthly themes for reflection.

- For groups that do not meet on an ongoing basis after returning, please use the themes provided, disregarding the suggested months.

- For groups who will gather a limited number of times after returning, we suggest picking the themes to look at together and then reflecting on the rest of the manual individually on an ongoing basis.

- For groups who gather once, we suggest a day retreat using different themes from the manual and then continuing to use the reflections individually.

- For groups who do not meet after returning, we recommend using the manual individually and emailing responses to each other or posting to a private social media group.

- For individuals who are not part of a group, we suggest using the book as it is designed and finding someone with whom to share your thoughts.

From Mission to Mission offers an additional resource for short-term mission, *Understanding Short-Term Mission: A Guide for Leaders and Participants*. See our website for more information: **www.missiontomission.org**.

Introduction

Welcome to *Remaining Faithful*, your companion for the next part of your journey.

Before we begin, it is important for us to say "Thank You." Thank you for giving the gifts of your time, presence, and talents to be with your sisters and brothers from another culture. Thank you for taking the risk to reach out and to be open to learning about people who may live very differently from you. You have done a great thing by taking time to experience a new culture and to use your energy and gifts to serve others. You will remember this experience all your life. You also have a unique opportunity to allow this experience to impact you and to inform decisions from now into your future.

Returning home is a very special step in the journey of anyone who has spent time in another culture. We know what this time is like because we are returned missioners ourselves. **From Mission to Mission** was founded in 1980 by a group of returned missioners who wanted to reach out and support other people returning home after having lived and served in another culture. Some of our members spent decades serving in mission, while others had shorter experiences which may have been similar to yours. We understand what you might be dealing with as you return home.

Perhaps you were part of a mission trip or sister parish exchange with your church, participated in an "Alternative Spring Break" sponsored by your school, traveled with a group of medical professionals to help people in need, or ventured on your own to work with the poor in a culture different from yours. You may have gone to a developing nation, to a rural or inner city area of your own country, or to a border area. Your time in another culture might have lasted a few days, weeks, or several months. Throughout this book, we will refer to your time in another culture as "your short-term experience."

Regardless of how much time we spent in another culture, we have all experienced the joys and challenges of returning home. We wrote this book as a support for you during the days, weeks, and months after you come back from your short-term experience. In these pages, we offer insights, ideas, questions, and suggestions for prayer and reflection based on our own experiences and the experiences of hundreds of other returned missioners who have worked with us over the years. We hope you find something here that will speak to your experience, ease your time of transition, and challenge you to further action.

As you begin this journey, we offer two suggestions to help you through the process. First, remember the importance of having the support of others as you tell your story, struggle with the questions, and seek out how God is calling you to be faithful to your experience. If you are not already part of a community, we suggest you create your own group or find a mentor who will share the journey with you; please contact **From Mission to Mission** if you need assistance with this step. Secondly, we encourage you to keep a journal, sketchbook, or notebook to record your thoughts and ideas during this reflection process. This book offers opportunities to write or draw about different aspects of your experience. Keeping a journal will give you adequate space to record your ideas and revisit them over time.

Oliver Wendell Homes wrote, "A mind that is stretched by a new experience can never go back to its old dimensions." We invite you to spend time thinking about how your short-term experience may have stretched you and helped you learn new things. You have completed your experience, but it does not have to be over. We hope this guide helps you discover ways to keep your short-term experience alive so that it becomes more than just a memory.

The first section of this book contains pages to guide your reflection each week for the first four weeks after you return. We suggest you set aside some time each week to read, reflect, remember, and talk about your experience. During this first month, we encourage you to make a point of remembering your time in another culture while all the details are fresh in your mind. After the first four weeks, this book presents monthly themes and moves into deeper reflection on the time you spent in another culture. We welcome you to set aside a special time each month to continue the reflection process, either alone or with a group, using this book as a guide. You might consider creative ways of using the materials, such as sharing your reflection process with others by email or through a message board.

We look forward to walking with you through this time. We know that we each have much to learn from our experiences and hope that this book will be a part of your journey toward remaining faithful to all that you gained from your time in another culture. Once again, we thank you for giving the gift of yourself. Welcome home.

Exercise

Hold your hands in an open gesture.

Then, close your fists tightly.

The goal of this process is to help you hold your experience in open hands so that you can continue to let it grow and speak to you. With closed fists, nothing new can get in, and we squeeze the life out of what we are holding.

Remembering Your Short-Term Experience

When was your short-term experience?

_____

_____

_____

_____

_____

Where did you go?

_____

_____

_____

Who else participated in the experience?

_____

_____

_____

What are some of the things you did during this short-term experience?

_____

_____

_____

_____

_____

_____

_____

_____

_____

_____

_____

WEEK 1
Welcome Home

Returning from your short-term experience, you may feel excited, exhausted, overwhelmed, or many other feelings. Allow the feelings to surface during this first week.

This is the time when you begin to share your story with other people in your life. It can be exciting to talk about your experience, and this storytelling is a key part of your initial days at home. Take time to enjoy sharing your experience.

Telling your story can also be challenging. Even though people want to listen, they may not be able to hear your whole story at once. During the time you have been away, other people have been busy here at home living their everyday routines. Though some may not be ready to drop everything and listen, it does not mean they do not care. Don't expect too much and you will not be disappointed by your efforts to share your story.

Remember

Thinking back on your experience, what brings a smile to your face?

Practical Things to Do This Week

- Review "Tips for Telling Your Story" on page 13
- Get photos developed and begin to share them with others
- Be sure to get plenty of rest
- Talk about your experience with anyone who is willing to take time to listen
- Journal, draw, or otherwise document your experience

Tips for Telling Your Story

- Be genuine. Be true to your ideals and your experience. Do not change elements of your story to seem more appealing.

- Reflect on where your listener is coming from. Ask yourself the following questions: Has this person volunteered or had a short-term experience before? What is my relationship with this person?

- Ask yourself: Are my parents/friends/coworkers ready to hear what I have to say? Don't judge.

- Be prepared that some people will need you to tell them the essence of your story in just a few minutes.

- Prepare different versions of your story for different audiences (a 2-3 minute version, a 10-minute, or even a 60-minute version to share with food and stories).

- Do not take negative reactions or inattentiveness as a judgment on your experience. You know the true worth of what you have lived.

- Understand that no one can validate or legitimate your experience for you. That important task is your responsibility.

- Ask God to be with you during this time, and trust in the Spirit's guidance. Know that you have your own good news to share, and take heart in the experience of the early disciples who spread the message of Christ all over the world.

—From St. Vincent Pallotti Center

PRAYER

Jesus told them, "Go home to your people and tell them what our God has done for you." Mark 5:19

Remember the people you met during your experience. Ask God to be with them, and pray for those who need special blessings. Thank God for your short-term experience. Remember those parts of your experience for which you are especially grateful.

WEEK 2
Treasure the Memories

Even though you have now been home for a little while, your short-term experience is still fresh in your mind. This experience meant a lot to you and may have impacted you significantly. At this very special time in your journey, enjoy the excitement and recognize all the feelings that may be associated with your experience.

While the experience is still so fresh for you, your family and friends may feel that they have heard your stories and are ready to discuss something else. Others might feel threatened by new things you share or feelings you express. It may be difficult to understand for those who were not a part of the experience. Be grateful when you find a willing listener.

As you return to all the details of your life, be aware that your short-term experience is becoming something of your past. For this reason, it is important to do something now that will help it live on in your present and future. Let this book guide you in that process.

Remember

Spend time with any photos you may have from your short-term experience. Remember the feelings and stories associated with them. Call to mind and to heart two or three memorable people from your experience, people whose images stay with you for some reason.

Practical Things to Do This Week

- Begin collecting items for your scrapbook such as pictures, postcards, names, quotes, facts, or words to songs and prayers
- Write thank you notes, as appropriate (host family, trip leader, donors)
- Continue to journal, sketch, or otherwise document your experience
- If you will be making any presentations about your experience, take some time to work on the content while the details are fresh in your mind

Rejoice with those who rejoice, weep with those who weep. Live in harmony with one another: live peaceably with all. —Romans 12:15-16

Who did you rejoice with and weep with during your short-term experience? What is your prayer for them?

WEEK 3
Your Feelings

By now you have told many people about your short-term experience. You are back into your routine, and life is carrying on as before—or perhaps life is continuing in a new way. During this time, you might have more opportunity and space to think about the time you spent in another culture.

Continue to be aware of feelings about your short-term experience that are surfacing. Maybe you are feeling blessed, excited, guilty, numb, exhausted, grateful, sad, joyful, angry, or other emotions. Make a special point of noticing these feelings.

One aspect of this type of experience is seeing things in a new way or learning something that you were not aware of before. Some people become more critical of themselves, others, their country, or their own culture. We encourage you to be honest with yourself about these feelings. You may want to journal about your feelings or share them with a trusted friend. Be cautious about sharing with everyone, as some may not appreciate or understand your new insights. New feelings are normal because you have experienced the world in a different way. Learn more about how to deal with these feelings and how to move forward with them in the Resources section beginning on page 48.

Remember

When you think back on your short-term experience, what feelings are you aware of? Journal about these feelings. Later in the process we will do more with those feelings. For now, just take the time to let the feelings surface.

Practical Things to Do This Week

- Create a scrapbook or photo album—include the most meaningful or interesting parts of your experience
- Find someone to keep talking with about the experience
- Continue to journal or draw about the experience
- Get back in touch with other group members
- If you are giving a presentation, continue to work on it

Let your feelings come forth.
Keep talking.
DRAW.
Journal.
FEEL.

. . . .

PRAYER

Like good stewards of the grace of God, serve one another with whatever gift each of you has received. Whoever speaks must do so with the strength that God supplies, so that God may be glorified in all things through Jesus Christ. —1 Peter 4:10-11

What new perspective or learning is a gift you received during your short-term experience? What in you needs strengthening so that you can share this gift here at home?

The Story Continues

It has been four weeks since you returned from your short-term experience. We invite you to look back on these weeks and ask yourself a few questions:

- What have you done or not done related to the experience? Why?
- What has been good or not good?

For some people, this may have already become a memory, a nice experience of the past. For you it might be more. In order to explore the deeper meaning and to have this experience become more a part of your life, additional reflection is necessary. Are you ready to go deeper? Are you willing to make a commitment to continue looking at the experience?

Who will you continue talking with about your journey? Our experience has taught us that it is important to have a mentor, guide, wisdom figure, or trusted friend to share this reflection process with you. We recommend that you invite someone to walk with you during this time.

Remember

Is there one incident from your short-term experience that you have focused on more than others? What is one thing about your experience that really stands out for you?

Who was your original source of inspiration to be part of your short-term experience? What would you like to say to them now?

Practical Things to Do This Week

- Continue to journal or draw
- Keep talking about your story
- Finish the scrapbook
- Invite a mentor to share your journey

PRAYER

I have learned to be content with whatever I have. I know what it is to have little. I can do all things through the One who strengthens me. —Philippians 4:11-13

What do you believe God is strengthening you to do?

As you continue to pray about your short-term experience, use the covenant on the following page to make a commitment to God and to yourself to look more deeply at your experience and to allow it to shape your life in new ways.

My Lord God,
I have no idea where I am going.
I do not see the road ahead of me,
I cannot know for certain where it will end.
Nor do I really know myself,
and the fact that I think I am following your will
does not mean that I am actually doing so.
But I believe that the desire to please you
does in fact please you.
And I hope that I have that desire
In all that I am doing.
I hope that I will never do anything
apart from that desire.
And I know that if I do this
you will lead me by the right road,
though I may know nothing about it.
Therefore, I will trust you always
though I may seem to be lost
and in the shadow of death.
I will not fear,
for you are ever with me,
and you will never leave me
to face my perils alone.

—Thomas Merton

Covenant

You have set off on a great journey. Now, we invite you to make a commitment to that journey by revisiting and reflecting on it each month. Are you willing to commit the time and energy to engage in this process? If so, take time to complete this covenant with yourself and ask for God's strength and guidance during your reflection process.

Loving God,

it is my desire to please you

in what I say and do in my life.

Because I believe that you called me

to my short-term experience,

I commit to continue looking at my experience,

to learn from it and

to live in a way that honors it and you.

On the _____ day of each month I will use this book to reflect on my short-term experience and how to integrate it in my life journey.

Signature _____ Date _____

God be with you on your journey!

MONTH 1
Going Deeper

As you begin your journey of monthly reflections, we are introducing a process for reflection called the "What?" model. This book offers several tools for prayer and reflection that help you look more deeply at the meaning of your short-term experience and its impact on your life as a whole.

See the Resources section on page 51 of this book for a complete description of the "What?" model. Read through the model and learn how the process works. The other resources in this book also contain suggestions for personal reflection. Review these methods, try them, and find what works for you. Each person is different and has different ways of reflecting, praying, and integrating the experience.

Each month, we will invite you to utilize the "What?" model to reflect on a particular aspect of your experience. Using this model to "unpack" your experience will be the focus of the remainder of this book. Keep in mind that you can also use the "What?" model at any time to reflect on or process different aspects of your experience that are not mentioned here. This is a tool; use it in the way that is most helpful.

What Does It Mean?

Pick something pleasurable that you remember from your short-term experience. Using that experience, work through all four stages of the "What?" model. See the sample reflections on pages 54-57 in the Resources section for examples.

Feast on the Experience

Who did you think about this month from your short-term experience? What were your feelings about that person?

Remaining Faithful

What have you done this month to remain faithful to who you have become because of your experience?

Questions to Consider

What questions are beginning to surface as you think about your experience? For example, "why do the people I met live so differently than I?" What changes are you aware of in yourself since your return home? Consider thoughts, feelings, prayer, attitudes, activities. What new insights emerge? Fill in the diagram below.

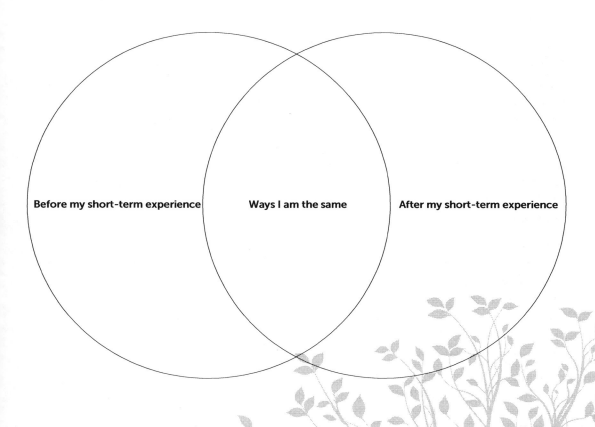

Before my short-term experience   **Ways I am the same**   **After my short-term experience**

PRAYER

From there Paul and Barnabas sailed back to Antioch. They gathered the people of the church together and told them about all that God had done through them.
—Acts 14:26-27

How did God work through you during your short-term experience? How will you share this with people you know?

MONTH 2
Gifts of the Journey

Many of us participate in short-term experiences to give something to others, to share our time and talents. Yet, we usually come back knowing that we received far more than we gave and that we will never be the same because of the many gifts we received.

Sometimes we might feel afraid of losing the experience, or returning to our lives and forgetting some of the profound lessons we may have learned. One way that the short-term experience can live on in us is by taking aspects of what we received and making them a part of our lives. This month, we focus on honoring the experience and the people we met. We acknowledge the gifts we received from witnessing how others live their lives and how they live their faith.

By becoming more aware of the gifts received, we learn to integrate the short-term experience into our daily lives. Only you know how you might have been changed by your short-term experience.

Feast on the Experience

Thinking back on your short-term experience, recall one person you are grateful you met because of the positive impact they had on you. Why was this person so important you?

Remaining Faithful

What have you done this month to remain faithful to who you have become because of your experience?

Questions to Consider

What have you learned from your experience that you hope never to forget?

What values did you witness that had an impact on you?

I hope I never forget ...

These values impacted me ...

What Does It Mean?

From the lists you made above, choose one value or insight, or a specific example that illustrates that value or insight, and use the "What?" model in the Resources section to further explore that topic.

· ·

PRAYER

To enjoy the fruit of your labor is a gift of God. —Ecclesiastes 3:13

People often say that they received far more than they gave during their time of service. What did you receive during your short-term experience? What did you give? What do you give thanks to God for?

Where Is God in All This?

As people of faith, we recognize that this experience may be very connected to your faith and your relationship with God. God is present through every part of your short-term experience and the things that have happened in your life since returning home. Short-term experiences such as yours are one way of living your faith, of putting your beliefs and values into action in the world in a concrete way. Take time to be aware of how God may be speaking to you at this time.

What Does It Mean?

Think back on your short-term experience. Choose one time when you felt the presence of God. Or, choose one time when you felt that God worked through you. Reflect on this part of your experience using the "What?" model in the Resources section.

Feast on the Experience

Who are the people from your short-term experience who helped you to feel God's presence or in whom you saw the face of Christ?

Name(s):

_____

_____

What did she/he do?

_____

_____

_____

_____

How did you recognize Christ in this person?

_____

_____

_____

_____

_____

What is God saying to you through this person?

_____

_____

_____

_____

_____

_____

_____

_____

_____

_____

Questions to Consider

How has your short-term experience become an ongoing part of your spiritual life? (For example, through prayer, meditation, worship or faith-sharing with others, or through ongoing service in some way.)

How has your short-term experience affected your relationship with God?

Remaining Faithful

What have you done this month to remain faithful to who you have become because of your experience?

PRAYER

After sitting down with them to eat, Jesus took break, said the blessing, then broke the bread and began to distribute it to them. With that their eyes were opened and they recognized Jesus, who immediately vanished from their sight. They said to one another, "Were not our hearts burning inside us as he talked to us ... ?"—Luke 24:30-32

When was your "heart burning within you" during your short-term experience or since your return? Just as you have reflected on God's presence during your short-term experience, continue that awareness in your everyday interactions with others.

Hurts

Most of our reflection so far has been on the positive aspects of your short-term experience. Now we will look at any painful aspects. This might include conflict with other group members, the pain of seeing other people suffer, or perhaps a traumatic or violent event that may have happened during the experience. Maybe you were disappointed about something related to your experience, felt disillusioned that things did not go as you had planned, or learned something that was difficult for you. Perhaps something happened at home while you were gone which was painful for you. There may even be something from your experience which you have not been able to talk about or share with others because it is hurtful in some way.

It is important to remember that God is present in our hurts and struggles. As Christians, we believe in the core message of hope. Jesus Christ reminds us that suffering and death are followed by resurrection and new life. We seek ways to make that hope real in the midst of our own pain.

There is only so much that we can hold on to from our experiences, and we do not want the negative or hurtful parts of life to take up that space and energy within ourselves. We are called to deal with the painful parts in a healthy way, by reflecting on what happened, acknowledging lessons learned, praying for healing and forgiveness, and moving forward in a new way.

Questions to Consider

Did you experience any conflicts with ... others in the group ... a person you met ... someone here who was not part of the experience ... God ... yourself?

Do you need to forgive or ask forgiveness of others or yourself?

Do you have any feelings related to disappointments, difficult things you learned, unmet expectations, or other challenges from your short-term experience?

What do you need to do so that you can move on from these difficult feelings?

What forms of violence or trauma did you witness? For example, physical violence, poverty, weapons, intimidation, living conditions, arguments.

Unresolved feelings about conflict and violence do not go away on their own.
If you need help dealing with feelings or experiences related to any of these questions, please consult the Resources section beginning on page 58. This section also contains suggested rituals you might use as a part of your healing from any hurts you may have experienced.

What Does It Mean?

From the answers to the "Questions to Consider," choose one specific experience of conflict or violence and use the "What?" model in the Resources section to further explore the issue.

Feast on the Experience

Where did you see hope in the midst of daily struggles?

Remaining Faithful

What have you done this month to remain faithful to who you have become because of your experience?

PRAYER

Jesus sent them forth ... "As for those who don't receive you, leave that town and shake its dust from your feet ..." —Luke 9:2.5

As Jesus explains to the disciples, things don't always go the way we plan. In order to move on with our lives, we need to let some things go by shaking the dust from our feet. Do you need to shake the dust from your feet regarding some aspect of your short-term experience? Ask God to be with you as you do this and seek the healing you need.

MONTH 5
Integration

"You don't know something is true unless it has changed your life." —Jim Wallis

All of our life experiences help shape who we are. You went on your short-term experience for some reason—feeling called, desiring to serve, sharing gifts, experiencing another people and culture. The experience and the lessons you learned from it are alive and can live on in you and who you will become.

Some of the ways we might change include our thoughts, feelings, attitudes, values, beliefs, understandings, actions, prayer, and relationships with God and others. Changes do not have to be drastic or major; the differences may be subtle yet still have a big impact on who we are.

What Does It Mean?

Think back on the time since you came home and identify one thing you did differently than you would have done before your short-term experience. Reflect on this part of your experience using the "What?" model in the Resources section.

Feast on the Experience

As you remember your short-term experience, identify a person or an event that impacted you in a way which might influence how you live.

Remaining Faithful

What have you done this month to remain faithful to who you have become because of your experience?

Questions to Consider

The following reflections may help you further understand any changes you may be experiencing and how you might live out those changes in your everyday life.

What changes are you aware of in yourself?

_____

_____

_____

How is your short-term experience impacting your life at this time?

_____

_____

_____

Who are the people you have related to differently since you came home? Why?

_____

_____

_____

Where in your life do you notice differences because of your short-term experience (home, school, work, church, community, friends, prayer, etc.)?

_____

_____

If you have not noticed any changes in your life, why do you think that is?

_____

_____

_____

When have you acted on something you learned during your short-term experience?

_____

PRAYER

Do not forget the things your eyes have seen nor let them slip from your heart all the days of your life. —Deuteronomy 4:9

What truth do you think God wants you to learn through what your eyes have seen from your short-term experience?

MONTH 6

Sharing the Gifts

We have looked at some of the gifts you received from your short-term experience. Some of the gifts of your experience may be challenges or risks you encountered successfully, such as learning to communicate with someone who speaks a different language or doing something you had never done before.

These gifts are not just for you to keep. We know that many people do not have the opportunity to be a part of an experience like yours. This month we are going to look more deeply at ways in which you may be called to share the gifts of your experience with others.

What feelings do you have about sharing the gifts of your journey with others?

What Does It Mean?

Remember a time when you told another person about something you learned during your short-term experience. Use the "What?" model in the Resources section to reflect on what it was like to share your experience with someone else.

Feast on the Experience

Remember one thing you did during your short-term experience or since then that you feel good about—a challenge you met, something you are proud of, a risk you took, a new experience, a new learning.

Remaining Faithful

What have you done this month to remain faithful to who you have become because of your experience?

Questions to Consider

1. What gifts have you received from your experience?

_____

_____

_____

_____

2. What have you already done to share your experience with others?

_____

_____

_____

_____

3. What would you still like to do to share your experiences?

_____

_____

_____

_____

4. What can you do to make this happen?

_____

_____

_____

_____

_____

PRAYER

In Luke 5:27, Jesus says, "Follow me."

"Vocation is defined as the place where your deep gladness meets the world's deep need." —Frederick Buechner

What vocation do you think might be your calling from God?

MONTH 7
Wealth and Poverty

During your short-term experience, you may have been exposed to ways of living that are very different from your own. Many people in the world have to deal with everyday realities such as poverty and violence that may or may not be a part of your own life. Your experience may have helped you see more clearly the contrast between the way your family lives and the way people live in other parts of this country and the world. This contrast can inspire many questions in us about the way we live and what we believe about our country, our faith, and how we live our lives. Let's take this opportunity to look more closely at some of those questions.

Questions to Consider

What are some of the differences you notice between your own culture and the culture you visited during your short-term experience?

My culture

_____

_____

_____

_____

_____

_____

_____

_____

_____

_____

_____

_____

_____

_____

_____

The culture I visited

_____

_____

_____

_____

_____

_____

_____

_____

_____

_____

_____

_____

_____

_____

_____

- What is one thing you appreciate most about the culture in which you live now?

- What did you see during your short-term experience that disturbs you?

- What is poverty? What is affluence?

- What is wealth, really?

- Where do you see richness in the culture you visited?

- How does your lifestyle reflect your values?

- What do you think your home culture could learn from the people you met on your short-term experience?

What Does It Mean?

As you remember the people and culture you met during your short-term experience, identify one thing that you find disturbing. Reflect on this using the "What?" model in the Resources section at the end of this book.

Feast on the Experience

One returned missioner said "We have lived with rich people who the world does not see as rich." Does this quote remind you of anyone you have met? Who?

Remaining Faithful

What have you done this month to remain faithful to who you have become because of your experience?

See pages 62-63 in the Resources section for ideas for further action.

PRAYER

This is what Yahweh asks of us, only this, to act justly, to love tenderly and to walk humbly with our God. —Micah 6:8

What is God asking of you now?

More Gifts of the Journey

In the second month of this reflection process, you began to look at some of the gifts you received from your short-term experience. Now, some time has gone by and we will look more closely at those gifts. Over time, gifts from your experience may have continued to emerge; today there may be more things you gained from your short-term experience than you may have initially recognized.

Questions to Consider

What were the stories that you told when you first returned? What really stood out for you initially as the gifts you had received during your short-term experience? Look back in your journal or on pages 24-25 of this book to remember some of your early reflections.

What memory from your experience stands out most clearly in your mind? What are some lingering images that are still with you?

Today, having had more time away from your short-term experience, what are some gifts of the experience that you may not have recognized initially?

Feast on the Experience

Think back on the one person from the culture you visited who you got to know the best. What would you say to that person if he or she were with you right now?

Remaining Faithful

What have you done this month to remain faithful to who you have become because of your experience?

Now that you have some distance from your short-term experience, what are some of the things you appreciate most about:

The other people with whom you served

_____

_____

The place you experienced

_____

_____

_____

The culture

_____

_____

_____

The people you met from that culture

_____

_____

_____

What gift is God offering you through these memories?

_____

_____

_____

_____

What Does It Mean?

Choose one experience from the thoughts above and reflect more deeply using the "What?" model found in the Resources section.

. . . .

PRAYER

Open my eyes so that I may behold wondrous things. —Psalm 119:18

What new wonders are you aware of? Thank God for them.

MONTH 9
But Why?

Short-term experiences often expose us to problems such as poverty, hunger, homelessness, violence, and other difficult social conditions. These issues can be hard for us to truly understand. We may feel motivated to do something to help the people who suffer, searching for ways to direct our time, energy, money, or prayers to change the situation. Helping in these ways makes a difference in people's lives, but it is also important for us to understand the causes of these problems, the deeper issues beneath the surface of the conditions we see.

Your short-term experience may have brought up many questions for you. Sometimes, our questions can make other people uncomfortable or challenge them beyond their current level of understanding. This is illustrated by the words of Dom Helder Camara, who said "When I give food to the poor, they call me a saint. When I ask why they are poor, they call me a communist."

If we really want to make a difference in a lasting way, we need to look deeply at the root causes of the problems we encounter. One way of doing that is to use a process called **But Why?** The following example illustrates how this questioning process takes us deeper into understanding an issue:

I saw a person picking through the garbage cans. **But why?**

He was looking for aluminum cans. **But why?**

So he could sell the cans. **But why?**

He needed money to buy food. **But why?**

He does not have a job. **But why?**

Because the steel mill closed down. **But why?**

Car companies decided to buy steel made in another country. **But Why?**

So they could make more profit. **But Why?**

When you reach a question you cannot answer, this is a place to do additional research, study, and personal reflection.

Questions to Consider

Think about something you saw during your short-term experience that brings up questions, something that disturbs you, or something that you do not understand. Write that experience in the first box, then answer the question **"But why?"**

▼

▼

But why?

▼

But why?

▼

But why?

▼

But why?

What Does It Mean?

Think about the situation you used in the process above. Now that you have a deeper understanding of it, use the "What?" model for further reflection on the issue.

Feast on the Experience

Think of one person you encountered during your short-term experience, or since you've been home, who you thought made a difference in some way, someone who gives you hope by their actions or attitude.

Remaining Faithful

What have you done this month to remain faithful to who you have become because of your experience?

· ·

PRAYER

Let us then make it our aim to work for peace and to strengthen one another.
—Romans 14:19

How are you called to live this out in your life today? But why?

Who Is God?

We have spent time reflecting on various aspects of your short-term experience. God continues to speak to you through this experience, and you continue to learn more about God as a result of what you experienced, your reflection on it, and how it is impacting your life. In Month 3, we looked at where God was in your short-term experience. Now, we are going to look more closely at who God is for you because of your experience. Your image of God may have changed or may be changing because of the people, situations, and ways of worshipping that you encountered in the culture where you served and since returning home.

Questions to Consider

Who is the God who has been revealed to you from your short-term experience?

_____

_____

How is this image of God different than before your experience?

_____

_____

_____

When were the times you struggled with God, doubted God, or felt distant from God? What have you done with these feelings?

_____

_____

When were the times you felt especially close to God? How did this feeling influence you?

_____

_____

_____

What do you know about God because of your short-term experience that you must proclaim to others?

_____

_____

_____

"Live in such a way that those who know you, but don't know God, will come to know God because they know you." (Author Unknown)

Who is this God? In your journal or on another sheet of paper, create an image of the God you have come to know as a result of your short-term experience. You may choose to draw, create a poem, write, or express your image in any other way that speaks to you.

What Does It Mean?

Recall an experience when you wish you could have had a conversation with God about what you saw during your short-term experience; use the "What?" model in the Resources section to reflect on that experience.

Feast on the Experience

Remember a time of prayer or worship from your short-term experience.

Remaining Faithful

What have you done this month to remain faithful to who you have become because of your experience?

PRAYER

For I am certain that neither death nor life—nor anything else in all creation—will be able to separate us from the love of God that comes to us in Christ Jesus, our Savior.
—Romans 8:38-39

How will you proclaim this truth to others during the coming month?

MONTH 11
Who Am I Now?

**"The highest reward for a [person's] toil is not what they get for it
but what they become by it."** —John Rushkin

In what large and small ways has your heart been transformed by your short-term
experience? Write those in the space provided below. Consider attitudes, beliefs, values,
skills, learnings, behaviors.

Questions to Consider

Because of my short-term experience,

I am more...

_____

_____

_____

_____

_____

_____

_____

_____

_____

I am less...

_____

_____

_____

_____

_____

_____

_____

_____

_____

_____

What Does It Mean?

Think about an incident, event, or situation from your short-term experience that changed your heart. Reflect on what you chose using the "What?" model found in the Resources section.

Feast on the Experience

Remember a time during your short-term experience and since then, when you have felt truly loved and accepted for who you are.

Remaining Faithful

What have you done this month to remain faithful to who you have become because of your experience?

PRAYER

The Spirit of our God is upon me, because the Most High has anointed me to ...
—Luke 4:18

How can you offer your transformed heart to God's people?

A Personal Mission Statement

**"Many of us arrive at a sense of self and vocation
only after a long journey through alien lands."**

—Parker Palmer

It has been a year since your short-term experience. Over these twelve months, you have gone through a process of reflecting on various aspects of your experience. At the same time, you may have done a variety of other types of service or volunteer work that you have also reflected upon and made a part of who you are. Our hope is that this book has been helpful for you to come to know yourself better, to know God more personally, and to live at home in a way that honors the people and culture you met during your short-term experience.

In this reflection process, we have helped you think of ways to integrate the short-term experience and the impact of that experience on your life. We hope you have identified some ways of remaining faithful to the experience. We encourage you to continue to use this book and the reflection models presented here as you continue to serve God's people in a variety of ways.

Our final activity focuses on writing a personal mission statement to support you in remaining faithful to who you have become as a result of your short-term experience. Use this mission statement to guide you, challenge you, affirm you, and support you as you continue to discern how to best be the person God calls you to be.

Writing a Personal Mission Statement

Your mission statement says the following about you:

- What your life is about
- What you stand for
- What you want to be remembered for
- What action you are taking to live out what you believe
- What God is calling you to do with your life

Your mission statement is not about your profession or about tasks to accomplish but focuses on who you are and how you want to live your life. Your work and other activities should then follow what is expressed in your mission statement.

A strong and effective mission statement has four qualities:

- Realistic
- Specific
- Flexible
- Simple

The eventual goal for writing a mission statement is to make it so simple that you can memorize it. Initially, you may need to write a longer statement explaining your values and who you are. Over time, you can continue to refine what you have written and eventually create a brief mission statement of one or two sentences that clearly expresses your personal mission in life.

As you meet new challenges and opportunities in your life, part of your discernment process could include looking at whether or not this new piece fits with your mission statement, matches who you are and who you say you want to be. Your personal mission statement thus becomes a tool for discernment and an ongoing guide as you move through the stages of your life.

This is our purpose: to make as meaningful as possible this life that has been bestowed upon us ... to live in such a way that we may be proud of ourselves, to act in such a way that some part of us lives on. —Oswald Spengler

---

In the space provided on the next page, begin to create your own mission statement. Use the points found on the bottom of page 44 to guide your writing process. Keep in mind Gandhi's saying:

"My life is my message."

My Personal Mission Statement.

_____

_____

_____

_____

_____

_____

_____

_____

_____

_____

_____

_____

_____

_____

_____

_____

_____

_____

_____

_____

_____

_____

_____

_____

_____

_____

_____

_____

_____

_____

_____

_____

"My life is my message."

As you conclude your journey of reflection you may wish to use this prayer individually or with your group to ritualize your commitment to remaining faithful.

Prayer of Sending Forth

Finally, my sisters and brothers, your thoughts should be wholly directed to all that is true, all that deserves respect, all that is honest, pure, decent, admirable, virtuous, or worthy of praise. Live according to what you have learned and accepted, what you have heard me say and seen me do. Then, will the God of peace be with you.
—Philippians 4:8-9

Questions for Reflection or Group Sharing

Who are the people you are most grateful for from this year?

What are the gifts of your journey?

Prayers of Petition

I want to ask God's blessing for...

I want to thank God for...

Blessing

Bless yourself or one another by tracing a cross on your forehead, ears, eyes, lips, heart, hands, and feet as directed in the following prayer:

Receive the sign of the cross ...

... on your forehead. It is Jesus Christ who strengthens you with this sign of love.

... on your ears, that you may hear and be guided by the voices of God.

... on your eyes, that you may see the glory of God every day of your life.

... on your lips, that you may speak of God's justice, peace, and love.

... over your heart, that the Spirit of God may dwell there.

... on your hands, that Jesus Christ may be known in the work you do.

... on your feet, that you may walk in the way of Jesus Christ.

As you go, remember to live simply, love generously, serve faithfully, speak truthfully, act peacefully, remember constantly, pray daily, and leave the rest to God. Amen.

Resources for Reflection and Integration

I.   Reflection Techniques

Creating Quiet Space for Reflection

In today's busy culture, finding space and time for quiet can be a challenge, yet empty time is something we all crave. Quiet space in our lives is also an essential component of prayer, reflection, and integration of our experiences. If we seek personal growth and greater depth in our relationship with God, we need time and space for that growth to happen. As a first step in creating more quiet in your life, try setting aside a few minutes each day just for solitude. Meditation or journaling can be ways to use this quiet time.

A Method of Meditation

1. Find a quiet place where you can sit and not be interrupted.

2. Sit still and relax your body. Pay attention to what is happening with your body. Feel the support of the ground or your chair. Quiet yourself.

3. Gently, begin to breathe more deeply. Be conscious of your breath. Breathe in God's goodness and breathe out everything that is not of God.

4. Let your breaths take you deeper inside. Try to keep your mind blank, or you may want to repeat a meaningful word or phrase to yourself. If you become distracted, gently repeat the word or phrase in your mind to refocus.

A Journal of the Journey

It has been said that the person who writes thinks twice. A journal can be a sacred place to hold memories, ideas for the future, special quotes, prayers, or songs that impacted you at a particular point on your journey. It is important for you to make your journal your own. You can write, draw, or use graffiti, which is a mixture of words and images. Use pens, markers, colored pencils, pastels, or other art tools that work for you. Consider the following methods:

- Think of a topic or person and just start writing words or symbols;
- Write the details of something you don't want to forget;
- Write a conversation that might happen between you and someone else, or God;
- Write the things you are grateful for from your day;
- Write about your feelings and other things you find difficult to share with others;
- Use pictures or symbols instead of or in addition to words.

When you are finished, go back and look at what you have recorded. What message might you discover to help you on your journey?

II. The "What?" Model:
A Process for Reflecting on Our Experiences

To help you look at and understand your experience, we will use a model of reflection called the "What?" model, which has been adapted from the work of John Borton. The "What?" model can be used to look at your whole short-term experience or a single incident that happened during that experience. For example, you might want to take time to reflect on an encounter with a particular person, the group you were with, the lack of resources you saw where you were, or poverty at a global level.

Overview of the 4 Steps

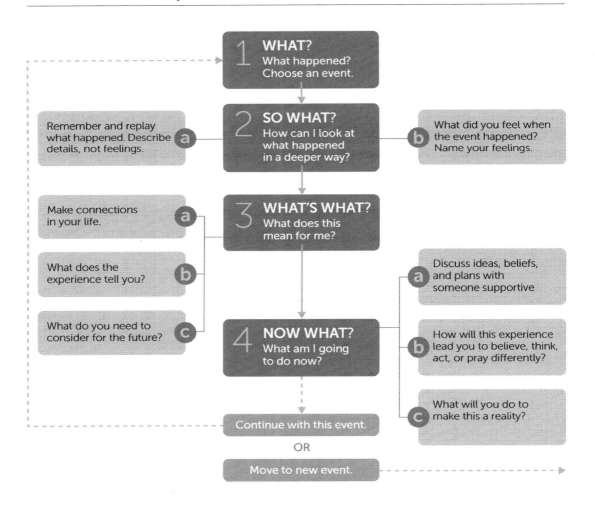

1. WHAT?
What happened?
Choose an event.

2. SO WHAT?
How can I look at what happened in a deeper way?
a Remember and replay what happened. Describe details, not feelings.
b What did you feel when the event happened? Name your feelings.

3. WHAT'S WHAT?
What does this mean for me?
a Make connections in your life.
b What does the experience tell you?
c What do you need to consider for the future?

4. NOW WHAT?
What am I going to do now?
a Discuss ideas, beliefs, and plans with someone supportive
b How will this experience lead you to believe, think, act, or pray differently?
c What will you do to make this a reality?

Continue with this event.
OR
Move to new event.

You can use this model again and again to reflect on different aspects of the experience or on any experience you have in life.

If this is your first time entering into a reflection process, see pages 48-49 for suggestions on how to prepare yourself to engage in quiet and meditation. Please follow these suggestions before each reflection activity.

The "What?" model has four components:

• WHAT? • SO WHAT? • WHAT'S WHAT? • NOW WHAT?

1. WHAT? What happened?

The first step is to decide what it is that you want to reflect on, spend more time thinking about, and come to understand better.

- Choose a relevant event, incident, or experience.
- Name it and write it down but do not include any information or details.

2. SO WHAT? How can I look at what happened in a deeper way?

Now that you've identified what you want to reflect on, it's time to look at it in a deeper way. In other words, so what?

- Go back, remember or replay what happened and your reaction. What about that event sticks in your mind? Describe the details using your senses but not how you felt. For example, who was there, what was going on, where you were, what it looked like. Avoid using feeling words.
- After remembering the details, focus on your feelings about the event, both then and now, so that you can understand its importance and meaning. Try to name your feelings as accurately as you can. Sometimes anger or sadness may cover up other emotions. It might be easier to recognize that you feel angry or sad; consider that you might also feel frustrated, guilty, lonely, betrayed, or some other emotion.

3. WHAT'S WHAT? What does this mean for me?

At this point you will look at what you have learned from the experience. You will make connections between your insights and feelings about the experience and other events that have happened previously in your life; or, you may not find any connections because what happened was so new for you. Although this step of the process can be difficult, it is very important, so take your time with it. Your short-term experience has provided you with new information that may show you a different way to think about things or even a new way to live. Reflecting in this way helps integrate these new insights into knowledge.

God called you to this experience. Let God speak to you through the wisdom of the experience. Please be open. This can be powerful!

Consider these questions and write or draw what comes to mind.

Making connections

- When have you felt like this before?
- Does this situation remind you of something you have heard before, a story you once read, something else from your life? What is it?
- What happened in that story or experience?
- In what way is it similar to and different from this one?

What does your experience tell you?

- What insights, values, attitudes, needs, and goals have become important to you as a result of your experience?
- What have you learned?
- What surprises you? What shocks you?
- Does this challenge your beliefs? How?
- Do your insights energize you? In what way?
- What do you think God is saying to you?
- What do you believe/think now?

What do you need to consider for the future?

- What do you want to hold on to from this part of the experience?
- What lessons do you always want to remember?
- Are you going to make new decisions based on this reflection? What?

4. <u>NOW WHAT?</u> What am I going to do now?

This final step helps you identify what action you will take as a result of your reflection. This action is how you remain faithful to who you have become. Perhaps your reflection has energized you to get involved in your community, to make a commitment to a particular issue, to make a change in your life, or to learn more about something. The following will help give you some direction.

A. Discuss new ideas, beliefs, or plans with someone who can support and guide you. Ask a wisdom-figure or mentor to help you put this new learning into action.

B. All of your reflection leads to this point. Each new experience we have helps us to grow and change. It is important to realize, as best you can, how you are different because of your short-term experience. How will this lead you to believe differently? To think differently? To act differently? To pray differently? The goal of reflection is integration...to remain faithful to who you have become. The challenge now is to act on the wisdom of your reflection.

C. For the above to become a reality, write the details of your plan to accomplish this action. What realistic steps do you need to take to make this happen? Consider:

- What are you going to do? When will you do it?
- Who do you need to contact in order to do this? How? When?
- What other factors do you need to consider? How will you deal with them?

D. Find others who have had similar experiences and share your vision of mission and service, people who can help you keep the experience alive. Consider talking with group leaders, other group members, church leaders, mentors, friends.

E. Reminders: connect with others; continue prayer and reflection; act.

The "What" Model—Example 1

1. What?

In Tijuana I noticed that there were many children on the street selling items like chewing gum and small toys. It caught my attention.

2. So What?

Seeing all those kids selling stuff just got me thinking. They were just kids hawking things to rich tourists in an ugly border town. They were on every street corner, trying to sell Chiclets, wooden toys, or simple jewelry. Some were just begging. They were all young. My 8-year-old daughter asked me why children her age were working like that in a hot and crowded street. We bought some things from some of them. And I remember seeing my daughter standing next to one of the street kids as she bought a woven bracelet. Just two kids standing together. The same but different.

It got me thinking—why were kids selling on the streets like that? Were they just making a quick buck from tourists? They were just kids. And sometimes I noticed the American tourists were not that kind to them. Maybe I treated them poorly, too.

So who set these kids up for this? Why did they have to do this? They didn't seem well dressed or well cared for. Even after leaving Tijuana I was still thinking about some of the kids and the fact that there were so many of them. I felt sorry for these kids, sad that they had to do this. Kids deserve the opportunity to be kids.

My kids were with me and what a comparison. They were having fun in a new and different place. I was uncomfortable noticing the contrast with my own life, how good it is, and how we have everything we need and more. I'm so grateful that I can take care of my children. I'm happy that my kids have an opportunity to have different experiences and to enjoy being kids. Shouldn't all kids have that chance? I'm struck by the contrast in the few miles between the affluence of San Diego and the poverty of the Tijuana streets. Why so much discrepancy in just a few miles?

3. What's What?

Making connections: When have I felt like this before?

I'm sad and upset when I hear about kids not getting to enjoy their childhood. Stories of neglect and the pain that kids experience get to me. Kids should not have to worry about their basic needs for care and shelter or love and basic safety.

What does my experience tell me?

It doesn't seem right that those kids should have to work and lose out on their childhood. It has made me think about the value of providing children with the opportunities they need to grow and learn and have their basic needs met. Kids in Mexico and kids in the USA. Kids everywhere. And it raises the big issue for me that I can't get out of my mind about why there is so much inequity in the world. All children should have the opportunity for a better future. Not just kids in Mexico, but what about the kids who don't have the same opportunities here in the USA? Kids with poor school systems or no access to health care? Why is that okay?

As a person of faith I truly believe we are all God's children and we are all equal in God's sight. There is no difference between us; we all have the right to fullness of life.

What do I need to consider for the future?

My thoughts and reflections about these children have brought the issues into focus. I need to learn more about the reasons for poverty and what I can do. Are those kids on the streets of Tijuana working because they have to? And what about kids here? What chance does a kid in the inner city have for a good education or for health care?

4. Now What?

These issues are important for me. What am I going to do? I need to find out more. Maybe I can talk to Fr. Joe who has worked in Mexico and learn about his experience. Maybe I need to learn about what the specific needs are for kids in the inner city here.

The kids in Tijuana started me on this process. At least I'll pray for them.

I'm going to talk to my daughter about what she thought and felt about those kids. I need to talk to my wife and share the thoughts that this process has brought forth.

Maybe as a family we should think about participating in our church mission trip next year. At least I should begin to talk about it. Maybe there's some action we might all take to make us more aware of the huge differences that exist in the world.

Maybe I need to learn more about the inequity that exists here in the USA with kids. What stops us from having better schools and health care for all kids? I'll read more about this and what the various political parties offer in their policies for the local area. Maybe our church has some connections too that I'll explore.

The "What" Model—Example 2

1. What?

A visit to a family in the neighborhood where we served.

2. So What?

When we got there the whole family was there in their two-room block house. They had fixed a huge feast for us, to thank us for coming. I had mixed feelings. I loved being with them. They were so good to us but I felt so guilty because I knew we were eating the food they needed to feed their family all week. I was kind of overwhelmed because they did this for me. I felt so honored.

3. What's What?

Connections: I used to think poor people were not good people or that they were lazy or didn't try hard enough. I used to think I was better than others because my family is wealthy enough to have a nice house and fancy cars and I can have anything I want.

When I think about that day I remember all sorts of sayings I've heard over the years that now sound different to me...Appreciate what you have...Finish your dinner; there are starving children in Africa who would love that...He'd give you the shirt off his back ... I received far more than I gave.

What does my experience tell me?

These people taught me that they are truly rich. If you have anything you have enough to share. I don't need most of what I have, and I should appreciate what I do have. When someone is so generous with their hospitality, it makes you feel amazing.

What do I need to consider for the future?

It was important for me to receive what they offered me. It was their gift to me.

4. Now What?

I need to talk to my grandma about what it was like to grow up in a poor family.

I will talk to others in my group to see if we could meet together regularly to talk about the trip and things we're involved in now that we are back.

I will remember this family we visited in my prayers.

I will show more respect to others, especially those I may have judged as not as good as me before.

I will pay attention to what I buy and try to limit what I buy to things I need. I will tell my family about this and invite them to do the same.

I will get involved with the poor in my area. I need to keep learning from them.

My Plan

I will call my grandma this week to tell her about the trip and let her know I have some things to talk to her about.

I will print some of my pictures and keep the picture with the family we visited on my dresser next to my prayer candle, to remind me to pray for them and to be more respectful towards others. I will write in my journal about this, too.

Today I will put a note in my wallet that says, "Do you really need this?" for the times I want to buy something. I will talk to my family about what I'm thinking and why and see if they want to join me.

By the end of the month I will talk to the social outreach coordinator at our church and the director of the volunteer connection about ways to serve the poor in my local area. After hearing the possibilities, I will choose one that fits me and sign up to get started by next month.

Notes

_____

_____

_____

_____

_____

_____

_____

_____

_____

_____

_____

_____

III. Suggested Healing Rituals

In Month 4 we looked at the difficult things that were part of your short-term experience. As you move further away from these experiences it is important to find a healthy way to carry these memories into the future. One way that we can deal with the "hurts" of our lives is through a healing ritual. Rituals are meaningful actions that help us express our feelings, or help us come to greater understanding. Our lives are filled with rituals, from a hug of welcome when you enter someone's home to lighting candles of remembrance. Here we suggest healing rituals to help you let go of that which you don't want to hold on to, or that which needs healing or forgiving, and giving it over to God.

"To surrender is to give over to God, to give up our power over something that keeps us down or holds us back. We trust that we will not be harmed and that letting go will be beneficial to our growth." —Joyce Rupp

- Write a letter to God expressing the "hurts" from your short-term experience. Bring this letter out where you can see it when you pray or carry it with you when you attend prayer or worship experiences. Put it away or destroy it when you feel that your heart has healed in some way.

- Write a letter to the person you are most upset with from your short-term experience and be honest with them about your feelings. When you have finished DESTROY THIS, and do what you can about making peace with those with whom you have been in conflict.

- Find a place outdoors where there are stones that you can safely throw. Think of the feelings you would like to let go of and throw a stone for each.

- Go for a long, hard walk/run/hike/swim/ride and ask God to help you release your feelings related to your "hurts."

- Find a quiet place where you can be alone. Get comfortable, close your eyes, and begin to breathe deeply. As you breathe out, imagine breathing out the negative feelings you carry and breathe in goodness and light from God.

- Go to a favorite place in nature. Pay attention to your surroundings. Feel the connection you have with God and God's creation. Ask God to help you see how everything in life is connected.

- Choose a special candle of healing. When you are feeling strongly about your "hurts," light this candle to remind yourself that the Spirit of God is always with you.

- Guided imagery: Use the healing exercise on the following pages as a ritual.

Remember, you don't have to deal with your feelings alone. Finding someone you trust to talk to is a valuable way to help yourself. If you continue to struggle with feelings of pain, disappointment, sadness, or other similar feelings, find someone you can trust and tell them. If you are a young person, it is important that you find a trustworthy adult rather than one of your peers. You may want to seek the advice of a counselor, mentor, or minister. Maybe God's healing for you will come through the gifts and skills of someone else. Be good to yourself.

Guided Imagery

For this exercise, you will need a household rag for each person. If you are alone, find a quiet, comfortable place to read the passage. If you are in the presence of others choose one person to read the passage. To prepare yourself, find a comfortable position, (if in a group invite the listeners to close their eyes while this passage is read) and take a few deep breaths to relax. Allow sufficient time at each (pause) for participants to imagine the situation.

Healing Rags

Imagine for a moment that you are at your favorite marketplace in the land you have said good-bye to. (Pause)

Look around and take in all the colorfulness of the different booths or shops and the crowd. (Pause)

Experience the different smells. (Pause)

Hear the voices of the merchants and other shoppers, maybe the chickens and dogs and music. (Pause)

Remember how you felt when you first went there...were you overwhelmed? Intimidated? Excited? (Pause)

Today your trip to this market is a special one. You are in search of something to help your heart. You have heard that there is a place in this market where you can get a special rag that heals hearts. You ask around and you are pointed to a place in the corner. You walk over weaving through the crowd. When you get there you find the most amazing woman, someone you have never seen before; it feels good just to be in her presence. (Pause)

She says to you, "I've been waiting for you. I'm here for you." How does it feel to hear that from her? (Pause)

Then she says to you, "What do you need today?" You do not know what to answer and say, "I've come for one of the healing rags."

She nods, because she knows why you are there. And then she tells you, "We have so many, let me tell you about them. We have rags like handkerchiefs, for soaking up the tears of sorrow and grief. This rag you can use as a bandage for tending to wounds and scars. Or we have rags that you can use as a tourniquet to stop the bleeding. We have some rags that are real thick...they're good for screaming into. Or this rag here, if you dip it in nice cool water it's just so soothing as it takes away the fever. This rag is good for polishing; it helps you see how good you really are. We even have plain old ordinary rags, to clean up the dirt that weighs you down and just makes you feel not so good about things."

You say, "So, what does this have to do with my heart?"

She answers you, "Everything! What does your heart need? Healing? Forgiveness? Comfort? Relief? Cleansing?" (Pause)

"Here's what you do, pick the one you need today ... take it home ... let it help your heart heal ...whatever ails you—give it to the rag—let the rag soak it up ... and when you feel like the rag has done its job you bring it back to me."

"That's it?" you ask.

"Well not really," she says. "When you bring it back I've got to wash it ... because you might need it again sometime ... because that's how life is."

You pick your rag, say your thanks and start to walk away. The woman calls out to you ..."You are not alone. I am with you always." (Pause)

You take her words and her healing rag, and you leave the market.

Take your rag and spend some quiet time thinking about what this rag represents for you. Think about how your heart needs healing and what you need the rag to do for you. When you are ready to let go of the rag and all that it stands for, let it go...put it in the washing machine, throw it away, put it in a sacred place. Once you let it go, you can't go back and pick it up again. Let it go means ... Let it go! Remember, you are turning it over to God. Only God can give us true healing and peace. "You are not alone, I am with you always."

Notes

_____

_____

_____

_____

_____

_____

_____

_____

_____

_____

_____

_____

_____

_____

_____

_____

_____

_____

_____

_____

_____

IV. Staying Involved

Now that you are back "home" you may decide that you want to live your life differently because of the people you met and all you learned. You might decide to make changes to your lifestyle or to be more conscious of the choices you make every day and how they impact our world. Perhaps you are ready to make a greater commitment to justice and peace, locally and globally. Consider these suggestions:

Stay connected to your experience and values through:

- **Prayer and spirituality:** Bring your care and concerns to God.
- **Stories:** Develop a few stories that illustrate key moments of learning from your experience that you can share when an opportunity arises.
- **Reminders:** Find a place in your life for art, crafts, photos, music, and food that remind you of your short-term experience.
- **Network and community:** Find others who share your values, beliefs, and lifestyle, as well as organizations that focus on issues you feel most passionate about.
- **Be informed about world and local justice issues:** Stay educated about the issues in your community, the area you visited, and beyond.
- **Connect with social teaching:** Research what your faith community teaches about social justice and find ways to practice it.
- **Life-long learning:** Continue to be open to learning, new ideas, and different ways to do things.
- **Live values learned:** Live in a way that honors the people you met and what you learned during your short-term experience.
- **Intentional living:** Be conscious of your values in the way you live each day and in how you make decisions.
- **Conscious choices:** Before making purchases, consider whether it is something you need or want; read labels on your food and clothing to see where and how they were made; whenever possible, buy fair-trade goods and ecologically sustainable products.
- **Meaningful action:** Find work or involvement that reflects your values and helps you feel that you are making a positive contribution to the world.
- **When faith becomes passion, things change:** Motivated by faith and reflection, together with others who share your vision, do something to positively impact an issue that concerns you.

Notes

V. Catholic Teaching on Mission and Justice

Documents of the Catholic Church: **www.vatican.va**

Ad Gentes: On the Mission Activity of the Church

Gaudium et Spes: The Church in the Modern World

Evangelii Nuntiandi: On Evangelization in the Modern World

Redemptoris Missio: On the Permanent Validity of the Church's Missionary Mandate

Centesimus Annus: A Century of Social Teaching

Evangelii Gaudium: The Joy of the Gospel

Laudato Si': On Care for Our Common Home

Statements from the U.S. Catholic Bishops: **www.usccb.org**

To the Ends of the Earth: A Pastoral Statement on World Mission

Teaching the Spirit of Mission Ad Gentes: Continuing Pentecost Today

Called to Global Solidarity: International Challenges for U.S. Parishes

Communities of Salt and Light: Reflections on the Social Mission of the Parish

Everyday Christianity: To Hunger and Thirst for Justice

Sharing Catholic Social Teaching: Challenges and Directions

From Mission to Mission **Services**

From Mission to Mission offers support to returning missioners, volunteers, and their sending organizations in the following ways:

Re-entry Workshops

Since 1980, intercultural missioners and volunteers have found the **From Mission to Mission** workshops a valuable part of their transition process. We offer two Re-entry Workshop formats for returning missioners and volunteers, a 10-day Workshop and a Weekend Workshop. Our workshops provide a safe place where missioners and volunteers are understood. The workshops focus on:

- Telling the story of the mission experience;
- Honoring the gifts of the experience;
- Recognizing what needs to be healed from the experience;
- Understanding re-entry and transition; and
- Integrating the mission experience.

Re-entry Resources

From Mission to Mission offers the following books for sale through our website:

Returning Home: A Guide for Missioners and Volunteers in Transition

Welcoming Them Home: A Guide for Families and Friends of Returning Missioners and Volunteers

Finding Life After Trauma: A Guide for Missioners and Volunteers and Those Who Care for Them

Remaining Faithful: A Guide for Reflecting on Short-Term Mission Experiences

Understanding Short-Term Mission: A Guide for Leaders and Participants

Consultation

From Mission to Mission staff is available to offer support and advice to individual missioners, volunteers, and mission sending communities and organizations at any phase of the mission experience—before, during, or after.

About the Authors

Julie Lupien has been the Executive Director of **From Mission to Mission** since 2002. In 2015, she received the first Pope Francis Mission Award from the U.S. Catholic Mission Association, in recognition for years of excellence, vision and compassion while ministering to missioners returning to the United States after both long term and short term mission engagements. As a member of the Volunteer Missionary Movement (VMM) Julie served in Zimbabwe, Africa and St. Kitts, West Indies. Julie's short-term mission experience includes Alternative Spring Break in Appalachia when she was a campus minister at Northern Illinois University, participating in the Young Neighbors in Action program in Yakima, Washington and a parish mission trip to St. Kitts when she served as a Pastoral Team member at Spirit of Peace Catholic Community in Longmont, Colorado.

Michelle A. Scheidt has worked in the nonprofit sector for 25 years and is currently a program officer at the Fetzer Institute. She served as a lay volunteer for two years and later co-directed the Claretian Volunteer and Lay Missionary Program in Chicago and served as a board member for **From Mission to Mission**. Michelle has extensive intercultural experience in inner city Chicago and in Latin America. She holds a BA in English from Marian University, Indianapolis; an MA in Pastoral Studies from Catholic Theological Union, Chicago; and a Doctorate in Ministry from Chicago Theological Seminary. Michelle and her spouse Barbara Crock live in the woods near Kalamazoo, Michigan.

From Mission
to Mission

missiontomission.org

Made in the USA
Middletown, DE
24 September 2018